WORLD WAR ONE

A SOLDIER'S LIFE IN
WORLD WAR ONE

Fiona Corbridge

W
FRANKLIN WATTS
LONDON•SYDNEY

🦇 Illustrations by
Mark Bergin
Kevin Maddison
Lee Montgomery
Steve Noon
Peter Visscher
Maps by Stefan Chabluk

First published in 2006 by
Franklin Watts
338 Euston Road
London NW1 3BH

Franklin Watts Australia
Hachette Children's Books
Level 17/207 Kent Street
Sydney NSW 2000

© 2006 Franklin Watts

Series editor: John C. Miles
Art director: Jonathan Hair

This book is based on
Going to War in World War One
by Adrian Gilbert © Franklin Watts 2000
It is produced for Franklin Watts
by Painted Fish Ltd.
Designer: Rita Storey

A CIP catalogue record
for this book is available
from the British Library

ISBN 0 7496 6495 9

Dewey classification: 355.0094'053

Printed in China

CONTENTS

HOW WAR STARTED

In 1914, the countries of Europe were on two different sides: the Central Powers (Germany and Austria-Hungary) and the Allied Powers (the Allies) – Russia, Britain, France and other countries.

When a Serb murdered an Austrian archduke, the Central Powers used it as an excuse to go to war. Austria-Hungary demanded Serbia's surrender. The Allies said they would help Serbia. A big war was on the way.

Murder
Archduke Franz Ferdinand was shot dead by a Serb in Sarajevo. This led to the war called World War One, the First World War, or the Great War.

WORLD MAP 1917

■ Allied Powers
□ Central Powers

PORTUGAL

Pacific Ocean

Canada

Britain

Russia

USA

Japan

Atlantic Ocean

Togoland

AFRICA

Dutch East Indies

India

New Guinea

Cameroon

German East Africa

New Zealand

German South-west Africa

Australia

ATLANTIC OCEAN

The war begins, 1914
The Central Powers go to war against the Allies. Germany marches through Belgium to attack France. Britain joins the Allies.

The war spreads, 1915
Germany uses poison gas against the Allies and attacks the Russians. The Allies attack the Turks at Gallipoli but do not win.

Western Front, 1916
There is a lot of fighting in the battleground of the Western Front in France. Many men die, but neither side wins.

NORWAY

SWEDEN

Jutland

DENMARK

NETHERLANDS

GREAT
BRITAIN

GERMANY

RUSSIA

Ypres

BELGIUM

Somme

Verdun

AUSTRO-HUNGARIAN
EMPIRE

SWITZERLAND

FRANCE

ITALY

ROMANIA

BLACK SEA

MONTENEGRO

SERBIA

BULGARIA

SPAIN

CORSICA

SARDINIA

GREECE

Gallipoli

TURKEY

ALBANIA

The two sides in WWI

• *The Central Powers
Germany and Austria-
Hungary. (Turkey and
Bulgaria join later.)*

• *The Allies
Russia, France, Britain,
Belgium, Australia,
New Zealand, Serbia.
(The USA, Portugal,
Italy, Greece, Japan
and Romania join later.)*

MAP OF EUROPE 1914

MEDITERRANEAN SEA

Allied Powers	Central Powers	········ Western front line of trenches 1914	Major battle sites
Countries joining Allied Powers	Countries joining Central Powers	Neutral countries	Sea battle of Jutland

The war at sea, 1916–17
British and German ships fight at Jutland. Neither side wins. The Germans use submarines to attack British ships.

America joins in, 1917
The United States joins the war on the Allies' side. Germany is outnumbered. The Russian army begins to collapse.

The Allies win, 1918
The Americans help the Allies to defeat the Germans on the Western Front. Austria-Hungary and Turkey collapse. The Allies win the war.

JOINING THE ARMY

In most countries, boys aged 17–18 years old had to serve in the army for up to two years. They were called conscripts. Countries did this so that if a war broke out, conscripts could be "called up" to fight and they would already have done some military training.

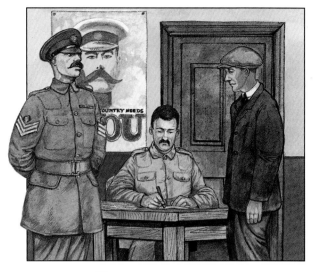

VOLUNTEERS
Many men who were not conscripts decided to fight for their country. In Britain, hundreds of thousands of ordinary men joined up.

A British infantry division
Infantrymen are soldiers who fight on foot. In World War One, the army was made up of infantry divisions. This British division would have had 18,000 men and 5,000 horses. It also had artillery (cannons and mounted guns).

Infantrymen

Machine gunners

Ammunition column

Royal Engineers

Howitzer brigade

Field artillery

Heavy artillery

Cavalry squadron

Supply train

Signals company

Medical section

EUROPE'S ARMIES

France
The French army was determined to attack the Germans as often as possible.

Germany
German forces were very well organized. They had officers called general staff who decided what the troops would do.

Belgium
Germany invaded Belgium in 1914 and conquered most of it. But the Belgian army carried on fighting for the Allies until 1918.

A QUICK WAR?

Many people had no idea what war would be like. They thought there would be just a few huge battles to decide who won. Unfortunately, they were very wrong.

The front
When soldiers spoke of going to "the front", it meant the area where the armies were fighting each other.

The front line
On the battlefield, the "front line" meant the troops that had moved forward and were closest to the enemy.

TROOP TRAINS
The generals on both sides wanted to get their troops to where they were needed as quickly as possible, so they used steam trains.

German troops going off to war by train in 1914

The French used 7,000 trains to take their forces to the front in August 1914.

THE WESTERN FRONT

The Germans started the war on the Western Front (a battleground in France and Belgium). They planned to capture Paris, the capital of France. But the French stopped them at the Battle of the Marne in September 1914.

Then the way of fighting battles started to change. Instead of using open land, soldiers fought from trenches.

THE BRITISH ARMY

Britain's army was small and could only send 150,000 men to France in August 1914, but they played a big part in fighting off the German attack. To get more soldiers, the British started a big campaign to persuade more men to join up.

BRITISH UNIFORMS

British infantrymen (ordinary foot soldiers) wore khaki uniforms which helped camouflage (hide) them from the enemy.

Infantry cap

British soldier, 1914

Tunic

Ammunition pouch

Lee Enfield rifle

Haversack

Entrenching tool for digging

Puttees (leg wraps)

Leather boots

EQUIPMENT

British steel helmet

German helmet

A soldier's kit

A soldier had to carry all the things he needed. He had food and water to last a few days, weapons, tools, a blanket for sleeping and a greatcoat to keep him warm.

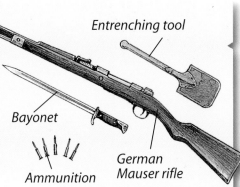

Entrenching tool

Bayonet

Ammunition

German Mauser rifle

Helmets

Exploding shells caused many head wounds. So soldiers were given protective steel helmets to wear.

German infantry kit

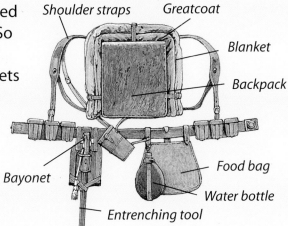

Shoulder straps

Greatcoat

Blanket

Backpack

Bayonet

Food bag

Water bottle

Entrenching tool

Weapons and tools

All infantrymen had a rifle. Soldiers could fix a blade called a bayonet to the end of their rifle and use this to stab the enemy.

IN THE TRENCHES

Soldiers were easy targets for artillery, rifles and machine guns. So they dug trenches in the ground to help protect themselves and fought the enemy from there.

FIELD ARTILLERY

In 1914, the most dangerous weapon was field artillery. These guns were easy to move and could fire quickly.

The French 75-mm gun was the best field gun. It could fire one shell every three seconds.

French 75-mm gun and crew

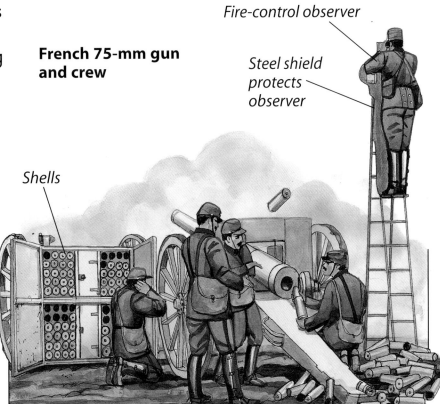

Fire-control observer

Steel shield protects observer

Shells

TRENCH WARFARE

By 1915, soldiers were fighting from trenches all over France and Belgium. In a battle area, each side had a front-line trench protected by rolls of barbed wire. Behind this was a support trench and then reserve trenches. They were connected to each other by communication trenches.

In a battle, the artillery fired lots of shells to start with. Then the soldiers went "over the top" (climbed out of their trenches) to attack the enemy. Many men were killed.

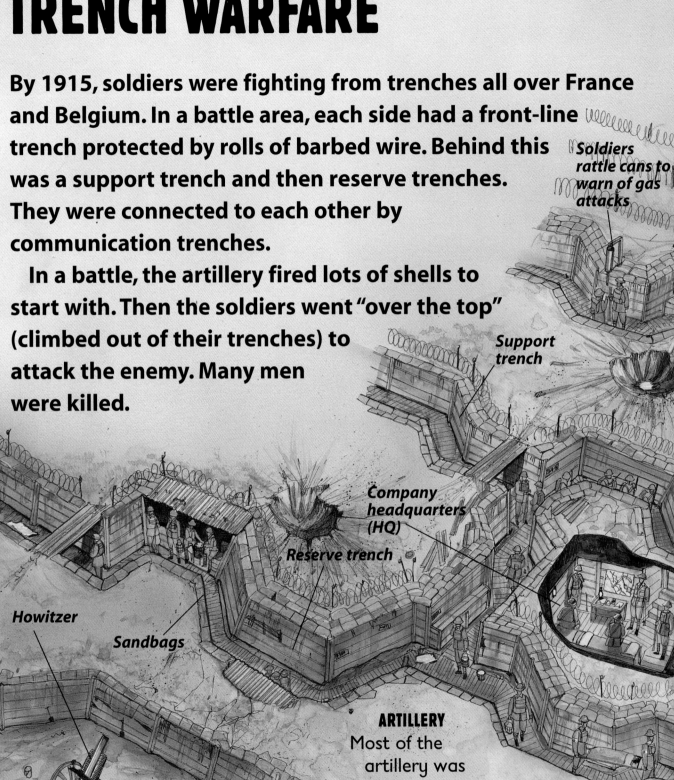

Soldiers rattle cans to warn of gas attacks

Support trench

Company headquarters (HQ)

Reserve trench

Howitzer

Sandbags

ARTILLERY
Most of the artillery was behind the trenches. Many howitzer guns were used. These fired heavy shells high into the air to crash down into the enemy's trenches.

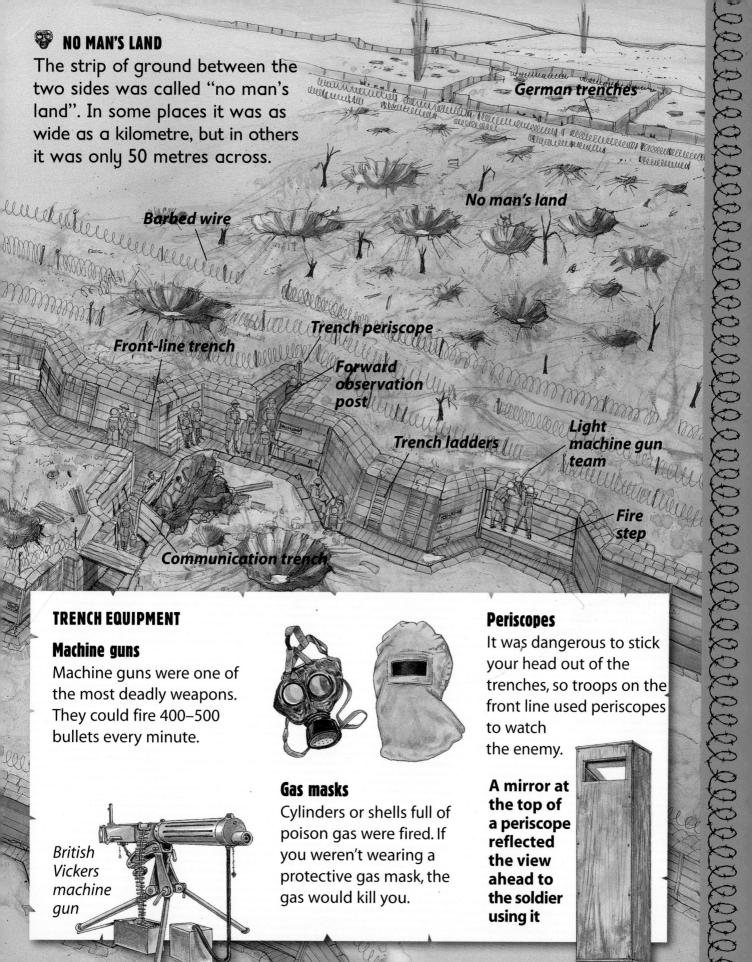

🕱 NO MAN'S LAND

The strip of ground between the two sides was called "no man's land". In some places it was as wide as a kilometre, but in others it was only 50 metres across.

German trenches

No man's land

Barbed wire

Trench periscope

Front-line trench

Forward observation post

Trench ladders

Light machine gun team

Fire step

Communication trench

TRENCH EQUIPMENT

Machine guns

Machine guns were one of the most deadly weapons. They could fire 400–500 bullets every minute.

British Vickers machine gun

Gas masks

Cylinders or shells full of poison gas were fired. If you weren't wearing a protective gas mask, the gas would kill you.

Periscopes

It was dangerous to stick your head out of the trenches, so troops on the front line used periscopes to watch the enemy.

A mirror at the top of a periscope reflected the view ahead to the soldier using it

WHAT WAR WAS LIKE

Living in the trenches was awful. There were plagues of rats. In wet weather the trenches soon became flooded.

Soldiers spent most of their time waiting to fight. It was usually too dangerous to move about in daylight, so they waited until it was dark to work on repairs and send out patrols.

ARMY GENERALS

Some people think that the generals who commanded the armies did not care enough about their troops, and that their battle plans caused many to die when it was not necessary. Millions of soldiers were killed or wounded on the Western Front.

French soldiers hang up their catch of rats

TRENCH LIFE

Life was boring in the trenches, so the soldiers sometimes had a little fun by organizing rat-catching competitions.

It was very difficult for the men to keep clean. Most of them had insects called lice living on their bodies. Men spent hours trying to get rid of the lice because their bites were extremely itchy and caused illness. But the lice always seemed to return. Lice caused cholera, a dangerous disease.

Germans wade through mud with a wounded soldier

💀 MUD AND SLIME

Rain turned battlefields into mud and made trenches collapse. The craters (pits) made where shells landed became great pools of slime. A man could drown in one in seconds. It became almost impossible to move supplies and guns.

Christmas truce
At Christmas 1914, a very surprising thing happened. In many areas, soldiers decided to hold a truce (stop fighting the enemy).

Soldiers from both sides met in no man's land and gave each other food. They even played football together! The truce lasted all day, and even longer in some places.

💀 TRENCH RAIDS

Both sides carried out raids in which soldiers dashed across no man's land to destroy a part of the enemy's trenches.

Muddy soldiers in a trench, sheltering behind sandbags and barbed wire

BEHIND THE LINES

Soldiers were allowed a short time to rest in military camps behind the lines (away from the trenches). There they could have a wash, change their uniforms and get a good meal.

Soldiers could take part in sports such as football, athletics and boxing. There was also entertainment to watch.

🎭 THE CANTEEN
This was a shop and a café where troops could buy things such as drinks, cigarettes and matches.

WORK AND PLAY

Maintenance
In the military camps, soldiers had time to mend weapons and equipment, and make sure it was working well.

Markets
Soldiers liked to spend their pay on food and drink. They often bought things from the local Belgian or French people. This soldier is buying mistletoe for Christmas.

Sport
The army liked the men to do sports because it kept them fit and healthy. Sometimes different units had competitions with each other.

HOSPITALS

The army set up many hospitals behind the Western Front to treat wounded soldiers.

Some soldiers had very bad injuries. Doctors sometimes had to amputate (cut off) limbs that were very badly damaged. The soldiers had to be helped to learn to live with their wounds.

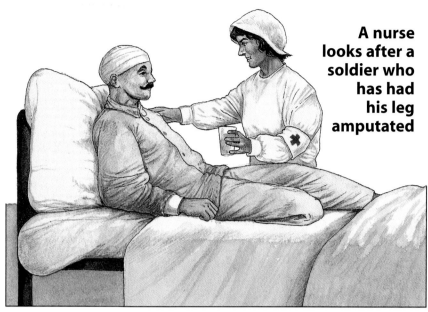

A nurse looks after a soldier who has had his leg amputated

ON WITH THE SHOW

The army organized entertainment shows for the men to enjoy and try and forget about the war.

Sometimes the soldiers put on their own shows. They dressed up in costumes (left) and made jokes about their officers.

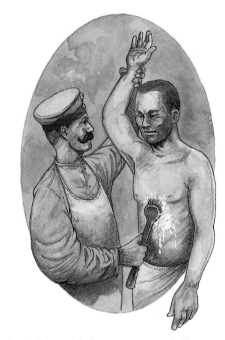

A helper delouses a soldier

KEEPING CLEAN

Soldiers arriving from the trenches were filthy and went straight to huge bathhouses to get rid of the dirt. They bathed in large tubs holding up to fifty men. Then they were deloused to kill the lice that had been living on their bodies. (Lice carried diseases.) Afterwards, they were given clean uniforms.

THE WAR SPREADS

The Allies went to war with Turkey in 1915. The Turkish troops were better fighters than the Allies expected. During 1915–16, they defeated the Allies several times.

But in 1918, the British army won many battles against the Turkish army.

Slang
Soldiers had lots of nicknames for things. Here are some:
- *British soldiers: Tommies*
- *German soldiers: Fritz, Boche, the Hun, Jerry*
- *Australian or New Zealand soldiers: Anzacs*
- *Britain: Blighty*
- *Artillery shells: whizz bangs, sausages, woolly bears*
- *Anti-aircraft artillery: ack-ack*

Australian and New Zealand troops land at Anzac Cove, near Gallipoli, in 1915

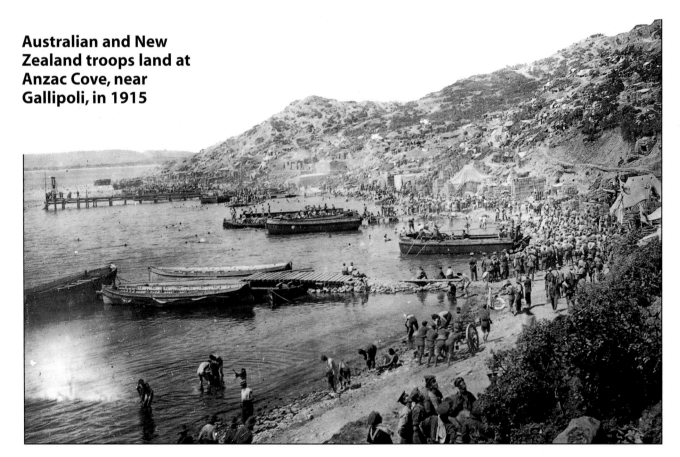

BEACH LANDINGS
In 1915, the Allies landed at beaches around Gallipoli to attack the Turks. But it was a disaster. The Turks fought hard and the Allies couldn't push them back from their defensive positions.

During the Gallipoli campaign, Australian and New Zealand troops fought with great bravery.

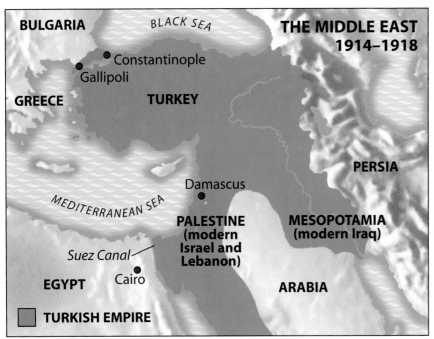

**THE MIDDLE EAST
1914–1918**

BULGARIA

BLACK SEA

Constantinople
Gallipoli

GREECE

TURKEY

PERSIA

MEDITERRANEAN SEA

Damascus

PALESTINE
(modern
Israel and
Lebanon)

MESOPOTAMIA
(modern Iraq)

Suez Canal

EGYPT

Cairo

ARABIA

☐ TURKISH EMPIRE

💀 TURKISH TROOPS

Turkish infantry soldiers were very tough fighters. They were trained by German officers. The Turks fought very hard until they were defeated in 1918. After the war, Turkey lost its empire.

A Turkish infantryman

💀 THE TURKISH EMPIRE

In 1914, the Turks had a large empire. The British were afraid that the Turks might invade Egypt and capture the Suez Canal. Britain needed to be able to sail along the canal to get to the East.

To stop the Turks getting control of the Suez Canal, the British invaded Palestine. In Mesopotamia, they forced the Turks to retreat (move back) along the River Tigris.

T. E. Lawrence on a camel

💀 LAWRENCE OF ARABIA

A British officer, Colonel T. E. Lawrence, was sent to help the Arab peoples fight the Turks. Lawrence led them in a guerrilla war in the desert.

Lawrence became a hero. He was known as Lawrence of Arabia.

THE EASTERN FRONT

The Eastern Front was where Germany and its ally Austria-Hungary fought against Russia. By 1917, the Russian army had almost been defeated.

In 1917, the people of Russia had a revolution and got rid of their ruler, the tsar. A new Bolshevik (communist) government got into power and signed a peace agreement with the Germans. This meant that parts of Russia came under German control.

Soldier of the Czech Legion

THE EASTERN FRONT 1917–1918
- - - - Front line, winter 1917
——— Front line, autumn 1918

RUSSIA

GERMANY

AUSTRO-HUNGARIAN EMPIRE

ROMANIA

BLACK SEA

AGAINST THE WAR

The Austro-Hungarian empire was made up of many nations, and some of them did not agree with the war. Czechoslovakia was one of these. It did not want to be part of the Austro-Hungarian empire. The Czech Legion was set up to fight for independence.

THE RUSSIAN ARMY

Russian soldiers fought with great bravery, but their commanders were not very good. They often didn't have the right weapons to beat the German army.

In 1916, equipment sent by the other Allies began to reach the Russians, but it was too late. The army collapsed in the following year.

Russian Cossack cavalry trooper

THE RUSSIAN TSAR

Tsar Nicholas II was the ruler of Russia. In 1915, he took over command of the army. But he was a poor commander. He was imprisoned and killed by the Bolsheviks in 1918.

The tsar inspects his army (left)

THE RUSSIAN REVOLUTION

In 1917, the Russian people were hungry and fed up with the war. They got rid of the tsar and set up a new government. Then the Bolsheviks took over. Russia left the war.

LENIN

Lenin was the Bolsheviks' leader. To get into power, he promised that the Russian people would have more freedom. But then the Bolsheviks made everyone do what they said.

Vladimir Ilyich Lenin

THE WAR AT SEA

The British stopped German ships from leaving or entering German ports. This was called a naval blockade.

The Germans used U-boats (submarines) to attack British merchant ships carrying supplies. They sank lots of ships. By 1917, the people of Britain had very little food.

WARSHIPS

Dreadnoughts were a type of battleship. They had heavy guns that could fire a shell up to 18 kilometres.

The ships were protected by heavy steel armour, which made them hard to sink. They had powerful engines and could move fast.

HMS *Royal Oak* fires its huge guns, which can swing round

BATTLE OF JUTLAND

The Battle of Jutland was fought in the North Sea in 1916. German Admiral Scheer hoped to trap part of the British fleet. But during the battle, the Germans were nearly trapped by the British navy, which was more powerful. The Germans realized that they were in danger, and managed to escape.

SINKING SHIPS

Submarines

German submarines (below) were good at sinking the Allies' ships. So to protect the merchant ships carrying supplies, the Allies got them to sail in large groups called convoys. Destroyers sailed as guards to fight off attackers.

Destroyers

The destroyer (above) was a fast warship. Its main job was to attack larger ships with torpedoes. It also had explosives called depth charges to drop on submarines.

Admiral Reinhard Scheer

Scheer commanded the German High Seas Fleet at the Battle of Jutland. Although the Germans had to escape, he said that they had won the battle because they sank the most ships.

THE LUSITANIA

The *Lusitania* was a British passenger liner. It was sunk by a German U-boat in 1915. Over 1,000 people drowned.

The United States was a neutral country, but some Americans died on the *Lusitania* and so the American people turned against Germany.

The *Lusitania* was sunk near Ireland

LEST WE FORGET

The Sinking of the Lusitania.

AMERICA JOINS THE WAR

Germany tried to make the people of Britain starve and surrender by sinking its supply ships.

Many American ships trading with Britain were sunk. German leaders knew that they were angering the

United States but decided to risk it. But in 1917 the USA sent a powerful army to France to help fight the Germans.

NEW WAYS OF FIGHTING

By the end of 1916, the armies on the Western Front had better weapons. They had light machine guns, mortars and tanks. Soldiers had more training and fought in small groups to help each other. Smoke shells were invented to hide soldiers as they closed in on the enemy. Gunners became good at firing artillery to land just ahead of their troops as they moved forward. This was called a "creeping barrage".

COMMUNICATIONS
Field telephones often stopped working in an attack. To pass on messages to their troops, officers sometimes used pigeons and dogs.

TANKS

The first tanks
The British army used tanks for the first time in 1916, but they were very slow. By 1918, tanks worked better and were more useful.

Armoured monsters
The German army thought that tanks were not much use, so they only built a few. The A7V tank had a crew of eighteen men.

Light tank
The Renault FT-17 light tank had a crew of two. It helped the infantry at battles in 1918. This tank was popular with American troops.

**A British tank attacks
German front-line troops**

💀 BATTLE OF CAMBRAI

The Battle of Cambrai in 1917 was led by tanks. They drove the Germans out of their trenches. But most of the tanks soon broke down or were destroyed. The Allies' attack was stopped.

💀 WAR UNDERGROUND

To blow up the enemy's front-line trenches (below), troops tunnelled underneath to set off explosives. If the enemy found out, they could dig a countermine to destroy the other mine first.

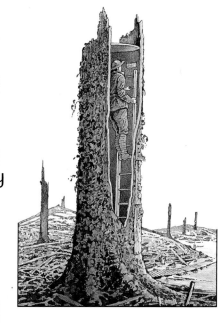

💀 FAKE TREES

Soldiers made fake trees to use as lookout posts. At night, they put them up next to real tree stumps then cut these down. Enemy soldiers didn't realize that anything had changed.

Allies' trench

Germans' trench

Allies' mine

Explosives

Germans' countermine

BATTLE IN THE SKIES

Air forces quickly got bigger during the war, and better aircraft were made. In 1914, Britain went to war with around 100 unarmed aircraft. By 1918, the Royal Air Force (RAF) had 22,000 aircraft of all types. People thought of pilots as heroes.

Aircraft were used to spy on the enemy, or to fight in battles called dogfights.

THE ARMY'S EYES

Spying on the enemy was called reconnaissance. Planes were ideal for this. They could see what the enemy was doing on their front line, and further behind it.

A British Sopwith Camel chases a German Fokker triplane during a dogfight

DOGFIGHTS

At first, pilots carried guns to shoot at each other. By 1915, planes had machine guns. They protected reconnaissance planes and shot down the enemy. Pilots who shot down more than five planes were called "aces". German Manfred von Richthofen shot down 80, Frenchman René Fonck got 75, and British pilot Edward "Mick" Mannock got 73.

AIRCRAFT

British

The SE5a was one of the best British fighters. It was armed with two machine guns and had a top speed of 202 km/h. It could fight any German aircraft.

French

The French SPAD fighter was very popular with French and American pilots. The SPAD XIII had two machine guns and could fly at more than 210 km/h.

German

Gotha bombers were used in raids on London and Paris. They carried up to 500 kg of bombs, but could only fly at a slow speed of 142 km/h.

AIRSHIPS

Both sides used airships. These were known as "zeppelins" because most of the German airships were built by Count Zeppelin.

Zeppelins were filled with hydrogen gas to keep them in the air. They were mainly used for reconnaissance and to bomb cities in Britain and France.

EDDIE RICKENBACKER

Eddie (above) was an American motor racing driver. He became a pilot in 1918 and soon began to shoot down lots of planes. At the end of the war he had shot down at least 26 enemy aircraft, making him the highest-scoring American pilot.

German Zeppelin L-50

THE ALLIES WIN THE WAR, 1918

The Germans sent all their troops to the Western Front for a last big attack. They did well at first, but the Allied forces were much bigger because the Americans had now joined their side. The Germans realized that they had lost the war and agreed to peace talks on 11 November 1918. This became known as Armistice Day.

An American infantryman, known as a "doughboy"

😷 THE US ARMY

The US army was small and not trained for modern warfare when it joined the war in 1917. But by the end of the war, it had over two million trained soldiers in France.

😷 GERMAN PRISONERS

German troops began to surrender because they were fed up with fighting and the Allies were winning. On a single day – 29 September – British troops captured more than 35,000 Germans.

A British soldier takes a German prisoner

EUROPE AFTER THE TREATY OF VERSAILLES, 1919

ESTONIA
LATVIA
LITHUANIA
EAST PRUSSIA
USSR
RHINELAND
POLAND
GERMANY
SAAR
CZECHOSLOVAKIA
AUSTRIA
HUNGARY
YUGOSLAVIA
BLACK SEA

🎭 TREATY OF VERSAILLES

This was an agreement to reorganize Europe after the war.

Germany had to give lands to the state of Poland and to France. The Austro-Hungarian empire was broken up into new states.

Czechoslovakia became independent. Lithuania, Latvia and Estonia were created.

🎭 VICTORY CELEBRATIONS

When the end of the war was announced, people were very relieved that the killing had stopped. In the Allied nations, people ran into the streets to celebrate. In the four years of the war, over 13 million soldiers had been killed.

A French soldier returns home

🎭 GOING HOME

Soldiers were now able to go home. But there were so many men in the various armies that it took a long time for this to happen. Many didn't get home until the end of 1919.

Celebrations in London
People crowded into the streets, dancing and singing. They waved flags, and blew whistles and hooters. Everyone was extremely happy that the war was at an end.

GLOSSARY

Turkish infantryman

Allies
The name given to France, Russia, Britain and Belgium, who went to war against the Central Powers. They were later joined by Italy, Greece, Japan and the United States.

Artillery
Cannons and mounted guns.

Blockade
Stopping ships carrying food and other goods from entering ports.

Bolshevik
A member of a Russian political party led by Lenin. It later became the Communist Party.

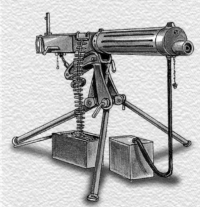

British Vickers machine gun

Campaign
The period of time when an army is fighting an enemy.

Central Powers
Germany, Austria-Hungary, Turkey and Bulgaria, who went to war against the Allies.

Conquer
To defeat and take over (for example an army or a country).

Defeat
To beat someone in a battle or war.

Defensive positions
Places where an army fights off an enemy attack. They are chosen to be as easy to defend (protect) as possible. For example, they might be on high ground.

Delousing
Using chemicals to kill insects called lice living on the body.

Eastern Front
Battleground in Russia where the Germans fought the Russians.

Field
An area where there is a military operation. Or equipment for use in the field e.g. field gun.

Field gun
A light artillery gun that fired shrapnel and high explosive.

Fleet
A number of warships.

Greatcoat
A soldier's heavy coat.

Guerrilla war
A type of war in which a small force makes small raids on the enemy.

Howitzer
A big gun that fired a shell containing explosives high into the air. It was very good for smashing trenches.

Independent
Not controlled by another country or power.

Invade
To go into another country or its land using armed forces.

Light machine gun
Ordinary machine guns were heavy, so the light machine gun was made. It could be carried by two men.

Infantryman of the Czech Legion

Lookout post
A place for keeping a watch on what the enemy is doing.

Merchant shipping
Civilian (non-military) ships that carried food and other goods from one country to another.

Military
Something that is to do with the armed forces.

Mortar
A simple and lightweight gun used by the infantry. It was like a mini howitzer.

Neutral country
A country that says it is not going to join in with a war.

No man's land
The strip of ground that separated the trenches of the two sides.

Patrol
To move around an area to make sure it is safe, or to see what an enemy is doing.

Reconnaissance
The way an army finds out about the position and movement of enemy forces.

Revolution
A rebellion against a ruler, government or political system.

Serb
A person from Serbia.

Surrender
To give yourself up to the enemy and agree that the enemy has won.

Torpedo
A long underwater missile.

Western Front
The battleground in France and Belgium where Germany fought the Allies. It had a line of trenches from the Belgian coast to Switzerland.

INDEX

PHOTOGRAPHIC CREDITS:
Mary Evans Picture Library p. 23
Hulton Getty Collection pp. 15, 18, 21, 29
Robert Hunt Picture Library pp. 9, 17